THE
NEW ORLEANS SAINTS

Copyright © 1981 by Creative Education, Inc. International copyrights reserved in all countries. No part of this book may be reproduced in any form without written permission from the publisher.

Library of Congress Number: 81-70277   ISBN: 0-87191-810-2

Published by Creative Education, Inc., Mankato, Minnesota 56001

THE NEW ORLEANS SAINTS

JAMES R. ROTHAUS

CREATIVE EDUCATION, INC.
Mankato, Minnesota 56001

The early years of professional football looked something like this. Fifty years later, in 1967, New Orleans finally got a franchise of its own. They called their team "The Saints."

New Orleans is a city of mystery.

It's a city of beauty.

It's a city of history.

The early French settlers fell in love with her. Napoleon was willing to fight for her. Americans were willing to die for her.

Today, a visitor to New Orleans is welcomed by a fun-loving people who are proud of their reputation for warm hospitality.

The annual Mardi Gras Festival, held each year in New Orleans, is a showcase for this hospitality. It is truly one of our country's most spectacular celebrations.

Bourbon Street, located in the colorful French Quarter of New Orleans, is a center of fine French-style cooking and Dixieland jazz.

And, of course, the mighty Superdome—one of this country's biggest and best domed stadiums — is the home of the New Orleans Saints, a team that has struggled through years of disappointing seasons. According to the experts, however, that long string of disappointments should soon be a thing of the past.

The Saints Come Marching In

In 1967, the people of New Orleans received the good news. Mayor Victor Hugo Schiro made the announcement: "The National Football League has decided that New Orleans is indeed a big-league city. Today, our proud city was awarded an NFL franchise!"

The passionate people of New Orleans received the news with their usual enthusiasm. They named the team the "Saints" in honor of the Dixieland song, "When the Saints Go Marchin' In." And they took the team to their hearts just as New Yorkers had fallen in love with the colorful Mets baseball team during the early pre-championship years. Parties were planned, and the welcome mat was rolled out for young John Mecom Jr. who, at 29, became the youngest franchise owner in the NFL.

Mecom was not only younger than the other owners, he had a maverick style all his own. At 6'3", 215 pounds, the handsome young cowboy/businessman from Houston, Texas was as big as most of his players. Mecom paid $8.5 million for the New Orleans franchise, and he was determined to get as close to the play as possible. At game time, you would find him down on the sidelines, sitting on the bench with his players.

In 1967 John Mecom, 29, became the youngest franchise owner in the NFL. The players called him, "one of the boys."

Tom Fears, the Saints' first head coach, held a rugged training camp that was described as, "a three-hour ride in a washing machine."

"If I had wanted a seat in the stands," he would tell reporters, "I could have bought one each Sunday for $6. I own the club and I want to be where the action is."

In the Saints' first season, Mecom found himself a little "too close" to the action. In a game between the Saints and the Giants, a brawl broke out among the players. When a few of the Giants ganged up on Doug Atkins, the Saints' popular 39-year-old defensive end, Mecom rushed out on the field to help his fallen player. Freeman White, a burly Giant, took a swing at Mecom with his helmet. Mecom ducked under the helmet and knocked White to the ground. That made Mecom the first owner in NFL history to score a one-punch knockdown over an opposing player!

Other than that one incident, however, Mecom was a perfect gentleman on the sidelines. And most of the players admitted that they enjoyed having an owner who was "just like one of the boys."

One of Mecom's first decisions as the Saints' owner was to hire a tall balding man named Tom Fears as head coach. Fears wore a big beautiful watch on his wrist — an award for playing with the 1951 Los Angeles Rams championship team. He also wore a gold ring on his finger — a token of appreciation for his work as assistant coach for the Green Bay Packers during the Vince Lombardi championship years.

Fears' experience under the hard-nosed discipline of Lombardi showed in the rugged training camps he held for the early Saints. One of the veterans complained that a session at a Tom Fears camp was "like a three-hour ride in a washing machine."

"If we win any games with the guys we have," explained Fears, "it will be because we're in better shape earlier than the other clubs. We want to know right away which guys can cut it. We haven't got time for the guys who don't want to hit."

Going into the 1967 season, the New Orleans Saints had a strange patchwork of unknown rookies and noble old veterans on the roster.

There was light-footed quarterback Gary Cuozzo, a four-year veteran who had been the back-up QB to Baltimore's legendary Johnny Unitas. Crowding Cuozzo were two other experienced quarterbacks — Bill Kilmer of San Francisco and Gary Wood of the New York Giants.

When rookie John Gilliam returned the opening kickoff of the '67 season for 94 yards and a touchdown, 80,000 Saints' fans went berserk.

Veteran Billy Kilmer (17) tore up the league in '69 by completing over 50 percent of his passes, most of them to clever Dan Abramowicz.

In the backfield there was veteran Jim Taylor, a bruising fullback who had made his mark with the Green Bay Packers. Next to Jim Brown, Taylor was considered the best fullback of his time. Though he never had Brown's breakaway speed, Taylor was ferocious up the middle. A handoff to Big Jim was almost always four yards in the bank.

On defense, Fears had drafted a trio of gritty linebackers from the Baltimore Colts. Jack Burkett, Ted Davis and Steve Stonebreaker had already played together, so Fears was confident they would bring solidarity to the young team.

From the Chicago Bears, Fears picked up two sturdy vets in Doug Atkins and Herman Lee, both in their late 30s.

"You need some old heads around to settle the youngsters," Fears said. "Atkins is still one of the best defensive ends in football. And Herman Lee will help where we need help most — in the offensive line."

Rounding out the first-year draft were several promising college picks, including husky Les Kelley, a 233-pound back from the University of Alabama, and speedy Don McCall, who had been Mike Garrett's understudy at USC.

By the end of the Saints' maiden season, many changes had occurred, most of them disappointing. The hope that had marked the early days of the draft drifted into despair as the Saints lost their first seven regular season games. Cuozzo, who had loudly demanded that he be given the starting QB job, had been traded to another team. That left Billy Kilmer in the quarterback slot. And, although Kilmer did his best, the inexperience of the team gave him fits.

A bright spot in the lineup was a little-known 17th-round draft choice named Dan Abramowicz. Though he wasn't even expected to make the team, Abramowicz fought his way into a starting receiver's slot, and proceeded to delight the hometown fans with his impossible catches — a total of 50 by season's end.

"He catches the ball on his knees, behind his back, anyplace," said Billy Kilmer. "He makes me look good, even when I'm bad."

Saints Fans "Best In the League"

Going into the 1968 season, the Saints had to be the least-respected team in the league. Jimmy Taylor, who had been the team's leading rusher with 390 yards the

Born with only half a foot on his right leg and no right hand at all, Tom Dempsey inspired the Saints with his awesome field goals.

The "miracle kick." Tom Dempsey kicks the famous 63-yard field goal with two seconds remaining as New Orleans defeats Detroit 19-17. The kick set a new NFL record. (1970)

previous year, announced his retirement from football. This left very little punch in the backfield.

Still, the lowly Saints were determined to give every team they played a run for their money. Playing the Saints at home was usually a bewildering experience, even for the toughest teams in the NFL. Part of the reason was the Saints' harum-scarum style of play. With nothing to lose and everything to gain, the team was never afraid to take risks or try something crazy — the blitz . . . the red-dog . . . the go-for-broke fourth down pass. You simply never knew what the Saints would throw at you next.

But it was the New Orleans fans who put a little extra pressure on the enemy. Usually, when a team gets off to a bad start, the fans stay home and watch TV. But not in New Orleans. In their first couple seasons, the Saints drew an average of more than 75,000 screaming, laughing, booing, cheering fans to each game.

"They have this love affair with their team," laughed Dallas veteran Pete Gent. "The Saints fans might boo a little bit, but they always come back laughing. I've got to rate them among the best fans in the league."

But football wasn't the only reason the fans showed up. Mecom had hired a guy named Tommy Walker from Disneyland to dream up the half-time shows. At one game, a giant Mary Poppins dummy floated into the stands amid fluttering clouds of free tickets. Another game saw a huge hot-air balloon soaring majestically past the press box. Still another game featured a thousand live pigeons and five thousand red-and-white toy balloons. The fans loved every minute of the pageantry.

Every game was the same. The New Orleans crowd hooted over the close calls — sometimes for ten minutes straight. Tom Fears nervously paced the sidelines, clipboard in hand. John Mecom sat on the bench with "the rest of the guys." And the New Orleans players pulled one strange play after another.

The result? The Saints made a good strong showing in every league game, beating mighty Pittsburgh 24-14 in the final game to finish third in the '68 Century Division. The Saints' two-year record of 7-20-1 was tops in history for an expansion team. And the fans had hopes for even better years to come.

Archie Manning could do it all. In 1972, he ripped enemy defenses for more than 3,000 yards and 20 of the team's 26 touchdowns.

Hank Stram took the coaching reigns in '76. Stram's system fit Archie Manning "like syrup on pancakes."

Kilmer Hangs Tough . . . Dempsey Kicks A "Miracle"

The years 1969 and 1970 brought more of the same. More close games. More exciting play. More pigeons and balloons.

The stand-out player in 1969 had to be old Number 17, the veteran Billy Kilmer. Billy was definitely Coach Fears' type of player. Other quarterbacks were bigger, younger, faster or stronger. But Billy was the guy who could always find a way to beat you.

"The league counted me out three years ago," said Kilmer. "But Coach Fears gave me another chance. It's a new lease on life. I have a chance to be a starter here, so I work harder than ever. I'm throwing better than I ever did in San Francisco because Coach gives me a chance to throw."

And throw he did! Although Billy played with a separated shoulder near the end of the '69 season, he had his best year by completing 53.6% of his passes for 2,532 yards and 20 touchdowns. Once again, his favorite receiver was the clever Abramowicz, who caught 'em high, low and on his ear. He was the NFL's best in '69 with 73 receptions for 1,015 yards and seven touchdowns.

All in all, the '69 season turned out better than expected. Though they lost their first six games, the Saints were in every contest. Then the offense went wild, winning two games by basketball scores of 51-42 and 43-38. These wins swept the team to their best season ever (5-9-1).

In 1970, New Orleans actually had two seasons. The Saints started out under Coach Fears again. After winning only one game of their first seven, however, Fears was replaced by J.D. Roberts of the Richmond farm team. What happened next will be talked about long after today's young football fans are old and gray.

On November 8, 1970, the Saints suited up to play their first game under the leadership of their new coach. Unfortunately, they were scheduled to play the powerful Detroit Lions, who were trailing the Minnesota Vikings by only one game in the Central Division. The Saints knew they were in for the battle of their lives, and somehow they kept the score close through the first three quarters. Amazingly, with only eight seconds left in the game, the Lions were leading by only one point — and the Saints had the ball!

With Manning calling the plays, the Saints reeled off three wins in a row, including a 20-17 victory over this man — O.J. Simpson — and the Buffalo Bills.

Coach Roberts held his breath as Billy Kilmer went to work. A sideline pass to wide receiver Al Dodd was good for 17 yards and brought the ball to the New Orleans 45 with only two seconds on the clock.

It was then that Roberts made an historic decision. With only one play left in the bag, Roberts sent Tom Dempsey, his 270-pound field goal kicker onto the field. The crowd was confused. They knew that the longest field goal in NFL history had been a 56-yarder. If Dempsey tried from this distance, the ball would have to travel 63 yards — a near impossibility!

If anyone could do it, thought Roberts, Dempsey could. Here was a man who had accomplished the impossible all his life. Born with only half a foot on his right leg and no right hand at all, Dempsey had grown up in Encilitas, California amid the cruel jeers and taunts of the kids in his neighborhood. They called him "Gimpy" and "Stumpy." But Dempsey was determined.

"My dad always told me that there was no such word as can't," said Tom. "And I proved he was right."

Dempsey made his mark as a high school tackle, sporting a shoe that had been cut in half and sewn.

At Palomar Junior College, Dempsey's coach encouraged him to give kicking a try. The blunt end of his funny-looking shoe actually made it easier for Tom to kick the ball. Dempsey had found his slot. At the end of his second year of college, the Green Bay Packers coaxed him away from school and signed him to a pro contract.

But now Tom Dempsey was standing out there on the field, surrounded by 70,000 fans who knew in their hearts that he had almost no chance at all to complete his mission. As teammate Joe Scarpati — a great holder — got set to receive the hike, Dempsey stared coldly down the field. From 63 yards away, the uprights looked like two little sticks in the breeze.

Never say can't. Moments later, Dempsey took his usual 2½-step approach, and buried his blunt right foot deep into the ball. The crowd swung their heads in unison as the football soared deeper . . . deeper . . . deeper.

"The gun sounded, ending the game, while Dempsey's kick was still soaring through the air," remembers sportswriter Richard Kaplan. "Players on both teams froze in suspended animation. They turned and gazed like tourists looking at the Empire State Building for the first time. They watched the ball carry and carry and carry — until, finally, it tumbled through the lower right-hand corner of the space between the uprights. The referee threw both hands into the air. The kick was good! Dempsey had kicked the longest field goal ever kicked in the NFL. The Saints had won the game 19-17."

Seconds after his record-breaking kick, Tom Dempsey — the man who never said "can't" — was carried off the field on his teammates' shoulders. Though the Saints would have to settle for another losing season overall, this was one moment of glory to be savored and remembered for years to come.

Archie Manning Receives A Hero's Welcome
The 1971 and '72 seasons would be long ones for the Saints, but there would be many high points provided by an exciting young rookie quarterback named Archie Manning. Archie, a star quarterback from Mississippi, was the Saints' number one draft choice in 1971. Kilmer had been traded to Washington in the hopes that a new field general might ignite a flame under the struggling New Orleans offense. Because Manning was a southern

Big Doug Atkins shows the raw power that made him one of the all-time great defensive Saints.

(1976) Rookie Chuck Muncie (42), an All-America from California, and Tony Galbreath from Missouri, gave the Saints a fearsome one-two punch.

boy, the fans welcomed him with open arms. And Archie was determined to earn his spurs.

In his first pro game, Manning took to the field like a man on fire. Though he was sacked and racked and jostled by the determined Los Angeles Rams defense, Archie guided his inspired teammates to a 24-20 victory — the Saints' first win ever over the Rams.

Later in the season, Manning did it again. Though things looked bleak in the late moments of a hard-hitting battle with Dallas, Archie pulled off some fourth-quarter magic to buy a 24-14 win.

Unfortunately, Archie was sidelined late in the season, and once again New Orleans slipped to last place in the Western Division.

The following year, hopes ran high as Archie roared back from his injuries in perfect shape. With the crowd spurring him on, Manning transformed himself into several quarterbacks at once. There was nothing he couldn't do. Passing? Manning ripped the enemy defense for 50 yards at a crack. Running? At times, he looked like another Fran Tarkenton, scampering up the middle, or rambling around end for another first down. In all, Manning accounted for more than 3,000 yards and 20 of the team's 26 touchdowns.

But football is a team sport, and no one player can be expected to pull the load by himself. Suffering from an unsteady front line, the Saints sunk to 2-11-1 by season's end.

Never Say Die

Though the Saints had experienced more than their fair share of losses in their first few years, the New Orleans fans never gave up on their team.

The years 1973, '74 and '75 saw the Saints building power, experience and depth.

In '73, a rugged ex-Marine named John North took over as head coach. His first two games ended in embarrassing losses. First, the Atlanta Falcons wiped out the Saints in the season-opener 62-7. The very next week, the Saints were manhandled by Dallas 40-3. But the Saints never gave up. They won four of their next six games, including a mind-boggling 19-3 victory over Washington.

In 1974, the Saints avenged their '73 loss to Atlanta by smashing the Falcons 13-3 on Atlanta's home field. The following week, the Saints surprised Philadelphia

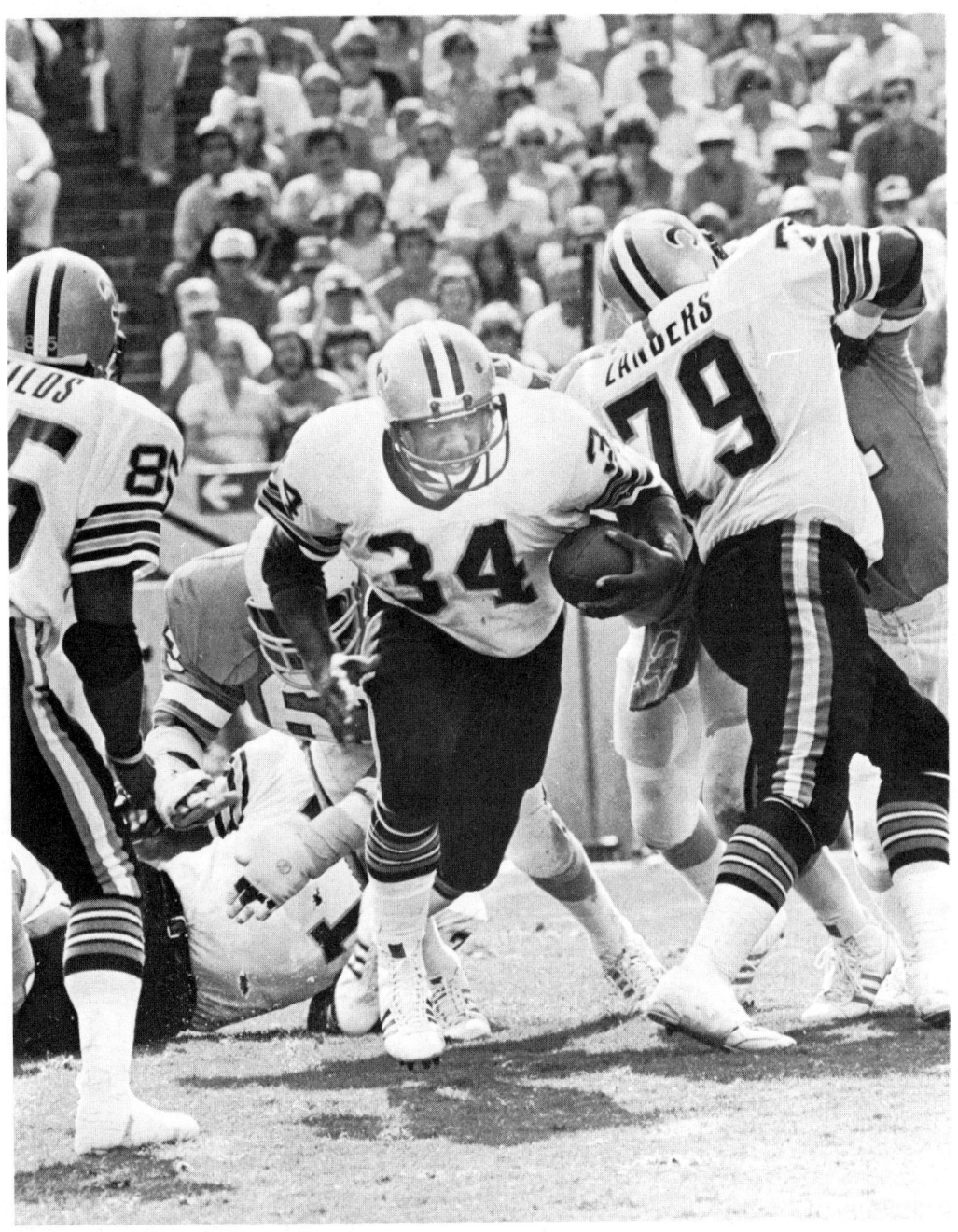
Fullback Tony Galbreath is good for at least four yards per carry — and is master of the one-handed flying end zone catch.

14-10 in front of thousands of ecstatic New Orleans fans. Then, on December 8, rookie quarterback Larry Cipa helped the Saints do it again by guiding his troops to a 14-10 route of St. Louis. It was the Saints' fifth win of the season, equalling their best record ever.

In 1975, the Saints lost momentum and coasted to a dreary 2-12 finish. All those losses aside, the folks in New Orleans still had something to cheer about. This was the year they moved into their brand new stadium, the spectacular Louisiana Superdome. Built at a cost of $163 million, the Superdome rises 273 feet into the sky, more than twice as high as the U.S. Capitol in Washington. With four scoreboards, six giant television screens and 76,791 indoor seats, the Superdome makes football viewing a treat. But, of course, a few more wins would've pleased the fans even more.

Hank Stram Takes Over

A few more wins. That's what Hank Stram had in mind when he was hired as the new head coach of the Saints in 1976. Stram, a fiery little man with a barrel chest, had been the best coach in the old American Football League. He had already guided the Kansas City

Hot receiver Tinker Owens (5'11", 170) is big play potential in a small package. Big things expected in the coming years.

Chiefs to one Super Bowl championship, and he hoped to use the same strategies to strengthen the sagging New Orleans offense.

"There will be a lot more action," Stram promised. "We'll be hopping around a lot, switching our line-ups to confuse the defense."

The Saints' first two draft choices were bound to help. There was Chuck Muncie, the All-America running back from California, and Tony Galbreath, the swift-footed back from Missouri.

It was Galbreath who rushed for 146 yards in Stram's first victory, a grudge-match win over his old team, the Kansas City Chiefs.

When the Saints trounced Atlanta 30-0 on October 10, the New Orleans fans went dancing in the streets. Another lopsided victory over Seattle 51-27 proved that Stram's strategy of "keeping the offense hopping" could certainly put points on the scoreboard.

The following year, 1977, the Saints' offense was bolstered even more when Archie Manning, one of the most exciting quarterbacks in NFL history, took over command.

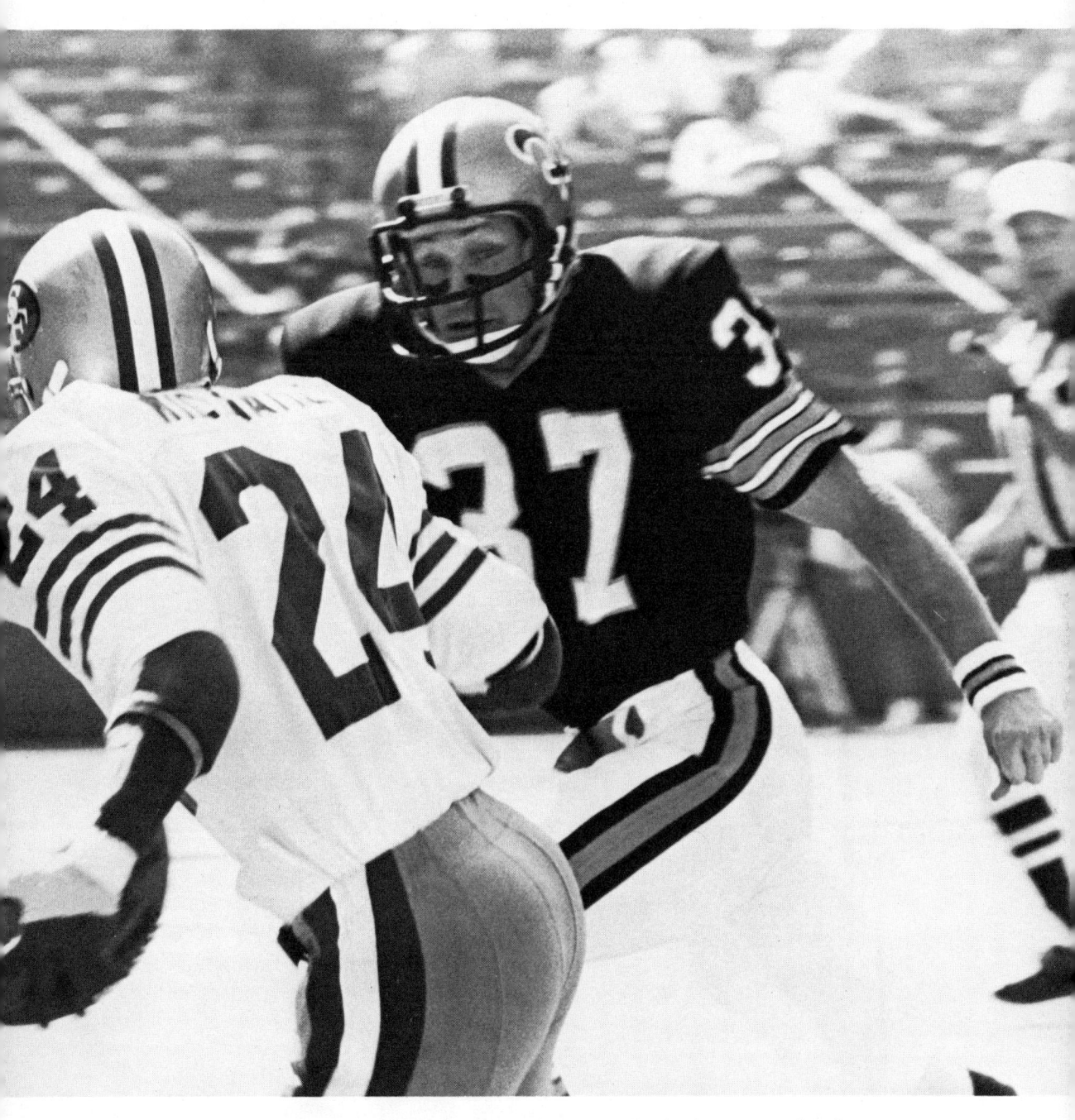

Free safety Tommy Myers is the Saints' career interception leader — second on the squad in tackles.

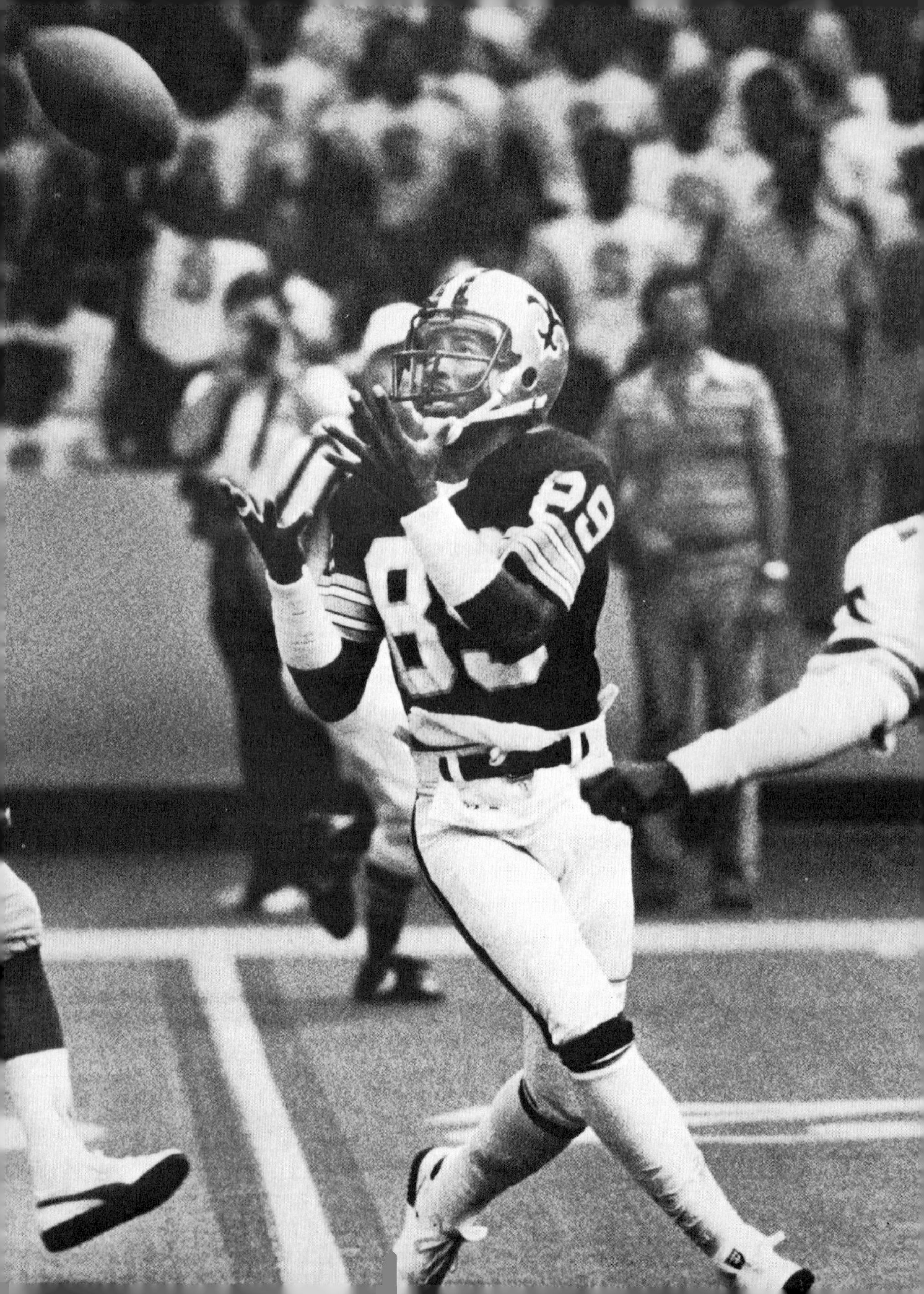

Manning, a red-headed, six-year vet from Mississippi, had spent a couple years on the bench nursing injuries. But he had used that time to study Stram's complicated offense.

"Archie works the system like syrup on pancakes," said Stram. "He's a lot like Lenny Dawson up at Kansas City — cool and smart — but he's bigger and stronger than Lenny. Heck, he's 6'3" and 200 pounds. And he moves like a big, smart cat."

With Manning calling the plays, the Saints reeled off three wins in a row, including a 20-17 victory over O.J. Simpson and the Buffalo Bills. It was the first time in the Saints' 10-year history that they had won the first three games of any season.

Can Nolan Do it?

Though the Saints seemed to be making progress under Stram, owner John Mecom surprised everyone in 1978 by firing Stram and hiring Dick Nolan in his place.

Nolan, who had won three NFC West titles as head coach of the 49ers in the early 1970's, was a quiet, smiling man with a face like an Irish leprechaun. He knew that the Saints had struggled through 12 losing seasons.

Wide receiver Wes Chandler has jet speed and vacuum fingers. He's full speed after just two or three steps.

And his goal was to strengthen the Saints' defense. His strategy worked — sort of.

In the early part of the '79 season, the Saints appeared to be playing the same old tune as years past. They lost four of their first six contests, including a 35-17 shellacking by the Rams in the Superdome.

And then — boffo! — suddenly the Saints came alive, rattling off three straight victories. For the first time in history, the Saints were the leaders in the NFC West — and, man, did it feel good!

"The only big games we used to have was when your grandmother came to see you play," bubbled Archie Manning. "Now everyone wants to see what the leaders of our division — us — will do next!"

There was no question that the Saints' new defense had made the difference. When New Orleans upset Washington, 14-10, they did it by stopping the Redskins 18 times without a score in goal-to-go situations. That night 3,000 New Orleans fans gathered at Moissant Airport to welcome the Saints home.

'They were chanting, 'Dee-fense. Dee-fense,' remembers Safety Tommy Myers. "It was a great feeling."

Bum Phillips, former Oiler head man, came to coach the Saints in '81.

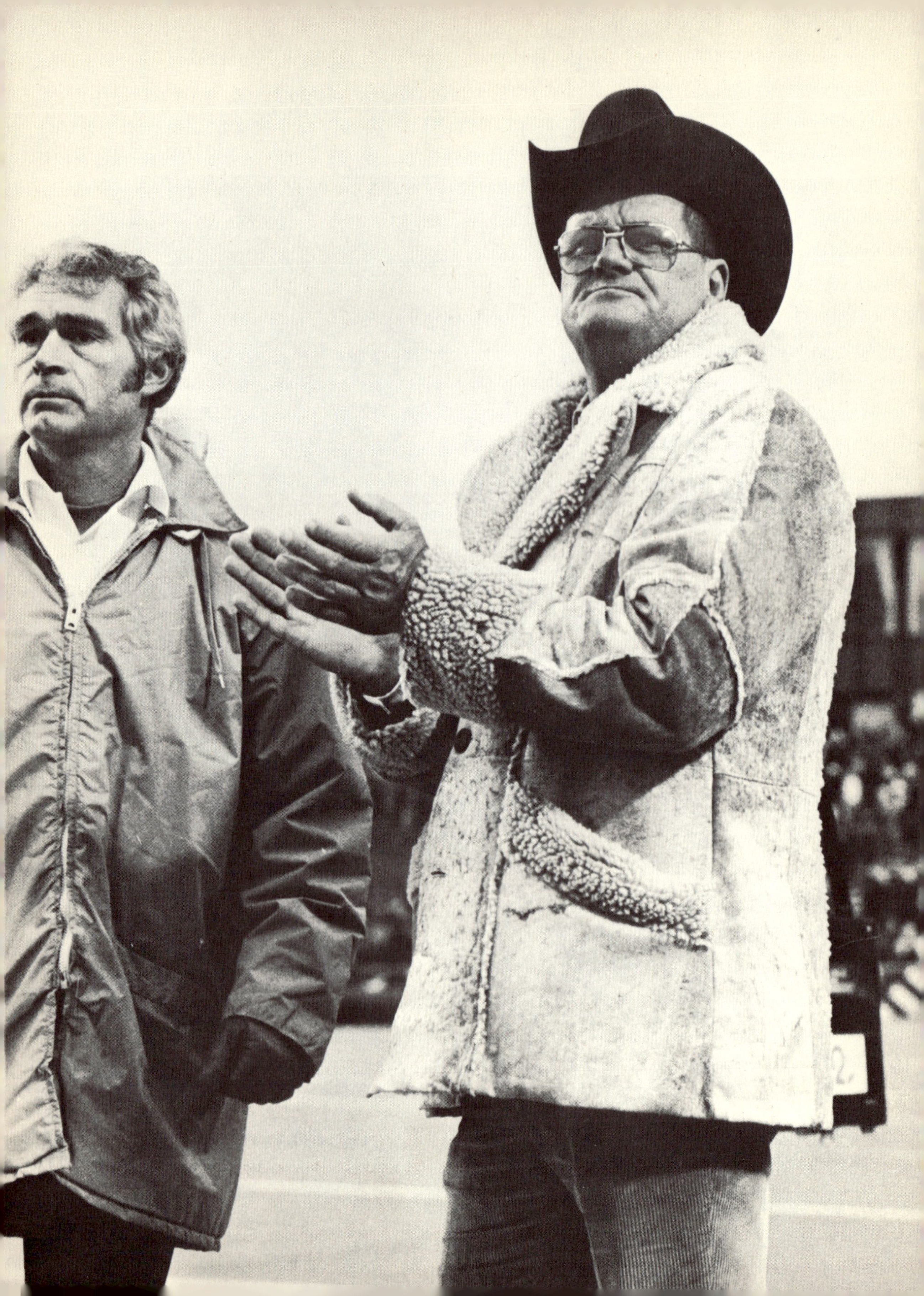

The 1979 season saw the Saints finishing 8-8, just one game behind the NFC champion Los Angeles Rams in the Western Division. It was the first time in the history of the team that the Saints could say they did not play on a losing team.

"We're getting close," said Joe Federspiel, the Saints' awesome middle linebacker. "We're gonna be there very soon. This town is dying for a winner. And everyone on this team is dying to be one."

The Year Of The "Aints"

If 1979 was a year to be remembered, 1980 was the year most Saints fans would probably love to forget. In sixteen games, the frustrated Saints managed only one victory — a 21-20 late-season squeaker over the Jets.

As the season wore on, sportswriters pinned a new nickname on the Saints by dropping the S. Some of the fans wore paper bag masks — a good-natured way of "hiding their shame" over the continued losses. And, of course, the players' morale was the lowest it had been in years.

Though the team could claim no real glory in 1980, individual players performed brilliantly at times.

Bum brings experience to the Saints. He led the Oilers into the AFC Championship game in 1978 and 1979 and reached the playoffs again in 1980.

Once again, quarterback Archie Manning was a standout performer. Six times during the year, Archie threw for more than 300 yards. His 301-yard performance against New England moved his 10-year career passing yardage past the 20,000-yard mark. In the end, Archie had set Saints season passing records for attempts (509), completions (309), yards (3,716), and touchdowns (23).

For his efforts, Archie was honored by his teammates as team and offense Most Valuable Player.

"When the season ended," said Archie, "I took a couple weeks, got away from football, and put our dismal showing out of my mind. I decided that I wanted to play. When Bum Phillips was hired, it cleared up the questions that I had about where the Saints were going and what my future would be.

The 80s Look Promising

The Bum Phillips Archie mentioned is the same colorful coach who took the lowly Houston Oilers from the bottom of the barrel to the top of the heap. Wearing his giant Stetson hat and lizard-skin cowboy boots, Bum led his Oilers into the AFC Championship game in 1978 and 1979 and reached the playoffs again in 1980.

It was this thundering running back — Earl Campbell — who helped put Bum Phillips' Oilers on the map.

Another Earl Campbell? "We're excited about George Rogers," says Bum. Rogers, the astounding 1980 Heisman Trophy winner, will help Bum lead the Saints into the '81 and '82 seasons.

As far as Bum is concerned, the Saints can rise from the ashes of the 1980 season and use their exciting new draft choices to help out the best of the returning vets.

One of those draft choices is George Rogers, the 1980 Heisman trophy winner who punished enemy teams during his sparkling career at South Carolina. Rogers stands 6'1¾" and weighs a powerful 224 pounds. He can run the 40 in a blinding 4.5 seconds. And it takes a Mack truck to bring him down.

"We're excited about Rogers," says Coach Phillips, "but we're pleased with our other boys, too.

"I'm not one of those 'wait until next year' people. I don't think that our fans expect us to win the Super Bowl right away. But I think they will see the type of football played that they like to see; a team that will go out and give an all-out effort, that doesn't surrender.

"My main objective is to put a team on the field that our fans here can be proud of. I think that sometimes you can be proud of somebody, even when they don't win. You can't win them all. But you can expect to compete in them all."

And you can bet that the proud New Orleans Saints will do just that.

The New Orleans Saints were founded in 1967 by John Mecom. On September 17, 1967, the team recorded its first regular-season victory. In 1979, the Saints tallied an 8-8 record — their best season ever. In 1981, former Houston Oilers coach Bum Phillips was named head coach of the Saints.

SAINTS RECORD, 1967-80

Year	Won	Lost	Tied	Pct.	PF	PA
1967	3	11	0	.214	233	379
1968	4	9	1	.308	246	327
1969	5	9	0	.357	311	393
1970	2	11	1	.154	172	347
1971	4	8	2	.333	266	347
1972	2	11	1	.179	208	361
1973	5	9	0	.357	163	312
1974	5	9	0	.357	166	263
1975	2	12	0	.143	165	320
1976	4	10	0	.286	253	346
1977	3	11	0	.214	232	336
1978	7	9	0	.437	281	298
1979	8	8	0	.500	370	360
1980	1	15	0	.062	291	487
14 years	55	142	5	.275	3,357	4,876

COACHING HISTORY

1967-70	Tom Fears
1970-72	J.D. Roberts
1973-75	John North
1975	Ernie Hefferle
1976-77	Hank Stram
1978-80	Dick Nolan
1980	Dick Stanfel
1981-	Bum Phillips